THE BRITISH MUSEUM
HOGARTH

Gulielmus Hogarth
Se ipse Pinxit et sculpsit 1749

THE BRITISH MUSEUM
HOGARTH

Tim Clayton

THE BRITISH MUSEUM PRESS

Frontispiece: Self-Portrait with Pug: 'Gulielmus Hogarth',
1749, etching and engraving (proof impression), 372 x 271 mm

© 2007 The Trustees of the British Museum
First published in 2007 by The British Museum Press
A division of The British Museum Company Ltd
38 Russell Square, London WC1B 3QQ
www.britishmuseum.co.uk

Tim Clayton has asserted his moral right to be identified
as the author of this work

A catalogue record for this book is available from the British Library

ISBN-13: 978-0-7141-5057-4
ISBN-10: 0-7141-5057-6

Photography by the British Museum Department of Photography and Imaging
Designed and typeset in Centaur by Peter Ward
Printed in China by C&C Offset Printing Co., Ltd

CONTENTS

Time Smoking a Picture,
1761, etched subscription ticket, 263 x 185 mm

INTRODUCTION

WILLIAM HOGARTH (1697–1764) was the first British artist to achieve worldwide fame., but he achieved celebrity through his prints, not through his paintings. This book contains a selection of reproductions of the most famous, taken from the British Museum's collection, which is the most comprehensive in the world.

Before photography, prints were the medium through which an artist's design reached a wide, international public. Since the invention of printmaking in the Renaissance, the new means of multiplying images had been employed regularly by painters who wished to make a name for themselves. As the influential French artist and writer Roger de Piles observed in 1699:

> Skilful painters who worked for glory, took the opportunity
> to make use of it to let the world know of their works. Raphael
> among others employed the burin of the famous Marcantonio to
> engrave several of his pictures and designs: and these admirable
> prints worked like so many figures of fame with his trumpet,
> which carried the name of Raphael to the whole world.

By the eighteenth century, having a design engraved on to a copper plate and then impressed hundreds or sometimes thousands of times on to sheets of paper was the normal, established route to a wider public. Like any other young artist aspiring to fame, Hogarth sought to make his name in this way.

William Hogarth was born in London, the son of a writer, an enthusiastic classicist who had come to London to make his fortune but failed and had instead ended up in confinement for debt. Hogarth was apprenticed at sixteen to Ellis Gamble, an engraver who specialized in incising decorations on silver plate. The boy, therefore, was taught to engrave, but not taught the subtleties of distributing light and distinguishing texture that he would have received from an engraver of fine prints. However, Hogarth was not inclined to settle for what he had been trained to do. Inspired by the ceilings that Sir James Thornhill was painting at St Paul's Cathedral and at Greenwich Hospital, he wished to become a great 'history painter', an exponent of the highest branch of art. In 1720 he set up as a jobbing engraver of shop cards, small illustrations and any other work that came along. At the same time he studied drawing, design and painting, using the facilities of Sir James Thornhill's academy and later also John Vanderbank's.

Both these men were champions of English art in opposition to foreign influences. They resented the habits of wealthy British patrons of bringing in French and Italian artists to undertake the most prestigious commissions, and of collecting old Italian and Flemish paintings in preference to modern work, especially contemporary English work. Affluent Britons were spending immense sums on art, but little of it was going to living Englishmen. English artists were struggling to reverse that pattern.

During the 1720s Hogarth invented and etched a number of small satirical prints, mostly directed against the great proponents of Italianate taste, William Kent and Lord Burlington. In 1725 he was commissioned by a pair of printsellers to design and engrave a British riposte to a highly successful set of French engravings, *L'histoire de Don Quixotte* (1723–4). His large 'Historical' subjects, as he termed them, were taken from Samuel

Hogarth's engraved business card, 1720

Butler's highly esteemed satirical poem *Hudibras*, 'The Don Quixot of this Nation'. This was Hogarth's first major venture into design and he was very proud of it. Towards the end of the decade he sold his first paintings and in 1729 he married Thornhill's daughter, Jane, without her father's permission.

However, it was the publication of *A Harlot's Progress* in 1732 that transformed Hogarth into a major artist with international acclaim. He envisaged a set of six prints that would tell a story. His twelve prints of *Hudibras* had visually told a story that already existed as a poem, but the *Harlot* was Hogarth's own invention. 'I have endeavoured', he wrote, 'to treat my subject as a dramatic writer; my picture is my stage, and men and women my players, who by means of certain actions and gestures are to exhibit a dumb show.' The engraver and art historian George Vertue was startled by the originality of this, 'the most remarkable Subject of painting that captivated the Minds of most People persons of all ranks and conditions from the greatest quality to the meanest'.

It was the financial success of the project that most impressed Vertue. This time Hogarth intended to cut out the retailers who had backed *Hudibras* and keep all the profit to himself. The increasingly wide circulation of newspapers offered new opportunities to entrepreneurs. By advertising in the newspapers read by potential customers, artists could now make direct contact with their public. James Thornhill pioneered this as a way of selling prints. It quickly gained favour with other designers and was adopted by Hogarth. He announced a subscription for a set of prints that would be completed in the future. Potential subscribers were invited to come and see the paintings at Hogarth's house. If they liked the paintings, they gave Hogarth their name and address, paid half the price of the prints in advance and Hogarth gave them an etched subscription ticket as a receipt. Newspaper advertisements kept subscribers informed of the progress of the project and eventually they collected their sets. To encourage subscriptions, Hogarth promised that *A Harlot's Progress* would be sold only to those who subscribed before 3 April 1732.

George Vertue had observed the progress of every project of this kind, but none succeeded like Hogarth's: 'these prints at a guinea a Sett had the greatest subscription – & public esteem that any prints ever had.' Hogarth's printer told Vertue that 1,240 sets had been printed, so Hogarth now had the names and addresses of roughly this many enthusiasts for his prints.

One aspect of the *Harlot's* reception left Hogarth with mixed feelings. Within a month of publication three leading printsellers were advertising a small set of copies for 6s., less than a third of the price Hogarth was charging. Thomas Bowles, another dealer, commissioned sets of copies in two different sizes, and within a year the set could also be bought printed in green. Before very long the Harlot's story could even be had as a large woodcut – the sort of print that adorned the walls of country cottages. Hogarth liked the idea of his designs permeating all levels of society and on other later occasions tried to publish designs in forms that reached those who could not afford to spend a guinea on a set of prints. He did not like the idea of other people profiting from his inventions, however. Exactly the same thing happened with his next print, *A Midnight Modern Conversation* (1733).

Hogarth was not the only designer to have suffered from having his own products undersold by piracies commissioned by printsellers. He and a group of colleagues got together to concert measures to defend themselves against such depredations. In February 1735 they successfully petitioned Parliament for copyright protection. Hogarth delayed publication of his second major series, *A Rake's Progress*, until June when the Copyright Act had come into force. The printsellers cunningly sent artists into his studio who designed sets of copies from memory. Thereafter, however, his copyright was not infringed.

In that year his father-in-law died and Hogarth used his equipment to re-open the lapsed academy for artists in St Martin's Lane. The academy provided facilities for drawing from life. It boasted several talented teachers of drawing and provided a generation of English artists with a very solid grounding. Hogarth constantly reiterated his belief that the study of nature was the artist's principal resource. *Time Smoking a Picture* (p. 6) contains his manifesto: 'To Nature and your Self appeal, / Nor learn of others, what to feel.' He rejected at once the grandiose theories, the veneration for old masters and the hierarchic establishment that was associated with the academies of Paris and Rome. Accordingly, St Martin's Lane was an egalitarian institution and its principles were thoroughly empirical. The later Royal Academy was set up on quite different lines, but many artists rejected both its structure and the theories of Sir Joshua Reynolds, and continued to adhere instead to the principles taught at St Martin's Lane.

Hogarth derived theoretical support for his own manner of painting from literary analogies. 'Prints should be prized as Authors should be read / Who sharply smile prevailing Folly dead' proclaimed the verse that accompanied his *Midnight Modern Conversation* (p. 31). He likened his prints to the satirical poems of the Roman, Horace, which made vicious and extreme behaviour look ridiculous, while holding up for admiration a middle way of moderation and humanity. In 1742, in his preface to *Joseph Andrews*, the author and Bow Street magistrate Henry Fielding likened his own branch of writing to Hogarth's 'comic history painting', deftly complimenting Hogarth with the remark that his figures 'appear to think'. Hogarth's *Progresses* and his larger, more ambitious, prints do not belong in a context of little political and ephemeral prints with which they are sometimes grouped. Their size, price and presentation put them side by side with the most ambitious prints of history paintings. His was modern, urban, English art, but art that claimed enduring seriousness.

In the 1740s Hogarth's Huguenot friend Jean Rouquet wrote explanations in French, then the international language, of Hogarth's best-known prints. The resulting pamphlet, published in 1746, contained useful explanations of local customs and circumstances on which Hogarth's comedy turned, for the benefit of foreigners who might not otherwise understand them. In future Hogarth enclosed a copy of the pamphlet with the increasing number of prints that he sent abroad. He often sold collections of his work; his self-portraits were used as the frontispieces, and the tail-piece that ends this book (p. 95) was designed to close such volumes.

He never ceased to champion modern art against what was foreign and old. *Time Smoking a Picture* mocks the idea that pictures that have the dirt and damage of time upon them are somehow better. He knew well that dealers could fake such effects. The subscription ticket for *Paul Before*

Paul before Felix, 1751, etched subscription ticket, 260 x 400 mm

Felix was a parody of an etching by Rembrandt, who was at that time the object of a vogue endowing his prints with what Hogarth considered to be absurdly inflated prices.

Hogarth occasionally painted and published subjects from literature and the Bible, but they were not received without criticism. It was his 'Modern Moral Subjects', as he called them, set firmly in contemporary England, usually London, that triumphed, not least as a way of painting for the present day. Indeed, one of the chief attractions of Hogarth for his contemporaries was that he was so startlingly modern.

A HARLOT'S PROGRESS

WITH *A Harlot's Progress* Hogarth began to explore previously uncharted territory. In six pictures he told a story set in contemporary London. Although the story was a simple one, understanding it depended entirely on the artist's ability to communicate meaning through the expressions of his figures and details in the pictures.

As the artist George Vertue observed, Hogarth was remarkably successful:

> He made six different subjects which he painted so naturally, the thoughts, and so striking the expressions that it drew everybody to see them — which he proposing to engrave in six plates to print, at one guinea each a set, he had daily Subscriptions came in, fifty or a hundred pounds in a Week — there being no day but persons of fashion and Artists came to see these pictures . . .

Those who liked the paintings enough to wish to buy a set of prints paid half the money in advance and were given a ticket. This was decorated with a scene showing a naked boy drawing an antique statue of nature and another boy engraving a copper plate, while a child satyr peeping up nature's skirts is admonished by a third boy. The satyr stands for the satirist. On the ticket Hogarth uses the iconographic language of history painting and the authority of the most highly respected Roman poets to justify what he sees himself doing with the *Harlot's Progress*. The quotation above is Apollo's instruction to Aeneas taken from Virgil's *Aeneid* to 'seek out your ancient mother' (nature). The quotation from Horace translates, 'A difficult subject must be presented in new terms . . . and license is allowed if it is used with care.' Hogarth claims to be presenting a new kind of art, treated in a new way. His goal is to depict nature, as authorized by Virgil. Satire requires him to explore her darker, concealed, sexual aspects. These might not normally be deemed respectable, but Horace justifies his approach.

Subscription ticket for *A Harlot's Progress: Boys Peeping at Nature*,
1731, etching, 148 x 121 mm

A Harlot's Progress was set in familiar, contemporary London. A very young, innocent country girl, identified by her chest as M.H. (later amplified to Moll Hackabout), arrives on the York wagon. At that date huge numbers of young people were moving into London from the country. She is met not by her cousin, for whom she has brought a goose as a present, but by a well-dressed woman. A lecherous-looking gentleman surveys her from the steps of the Bell Inn. Hogarth authorized a copy of this print which identified the woman as Elizabeth Needham, the notorious keeper of one of the capital's most fashionable brothels in Park Street, St James's, and the leering man as Colonel Francis Charteris. The contemporary explanation was that Needham was procuring promising girls for Charteris. Charteris had been condemned to death for the rape of a servant but pardoned thanks to the intercession of the prime minister, Sir Robert Walpole. He died anyway in February 1732, two months before the print appeared, and Needham in 1731 after being pilloried. The clergyman behind her might have protected the girl from this encounter, but he is wholly preoccupied with finding the address of a bishop.

A Harlot's Progress, plate 1, 1732, etching and engraving, 315 x 393 mm

a Harlots Progress Plate 1.

17

LEAVING BOTH Charteris and Needham's brothel behind, Moll has made a conventional career advance into 'high keeping'. She is now a sophisticated girl of seventeen or so, and a rich Jewish merchant has put her into a lavishly furnished apartment. He has just arrived unexpectedly and inconveniently. Having affected a loose *dishabille*, she demands the merchant's immediate attention and kicks over the coffee table. The distraction serves to cover the retreat of her young lover, who has put on most of his clothes while behind the curtains of her bed and now tiptoes to the door. They had been at a masquerade, for a mask lies on her dressing table. She has all the appurtenances of new wealth: delicate china, a monkey and a black servant. The room is decorated in the very latest early rococo style, and ornamented with dingy old master paintings of Old Testament subjects in frames that match the coffee table rather than the pictures.

A Harlot's Progress, plate 2,
1732, etching and engraving, 310 x 378 mm

Plate 2.

W. Hogarth inv. pinx. et sculp.

HOGARTH'S PRINTS were made with a combination of etching and engraving. A thin layer of wax was laid over the copper plate, which was then smoked. The artist drew freely on the wax with a needle, exposing the copper as he did so. His design appeared red on black. He washed the plate with acid, which bit into the exposed copper. With the main outlines in place, the wax was removed and the textures and shading were added in engraving. The plate was placed on a bag of sand and turned against the resistance of a wedge-shaped tool called a burin. The width and depth of the cut determined how much ink the line would hold and so how dark or light it would be. Getting this right demanded years of practice under the eye of a skilled professional, a training Hogarth had not been given.

The judicious combination of processes allowed for freedom of drawing, a great range and subtlety of tone, and fantastic scope for detail. The distribution of light and shade was the great skill. Different patterns of lines defined various textures such as silk, rock, water and flesh was handled with great delicacy, sometimes with dots.

Hogarth's prints are very largely etched. He made the most of his skill in drawing and did not entirely trust his ability with a burin in which he had limited training. When a plate absolutely required advanced skills he employed a fully trained fine art engraver to finish it. Nevertheless, his own skill as a printmaker was quite sufficient to produce clean, clear, legible and expressive results.

Detail of *A Harlot's Progress*, plate 2

Plate 3.

W. Hogarth inv.^t pinx.^t et sculp.^t

AFTER ONE ESCAPADE too many, perhaps, Moll has lost the Jew's protection. She has put on a little weight – possibly she is pregnant – and is operating on her own account in London's notorious red-light hot spot, Drury Lane. She is getting up after a hard night's work, just before midday, the time displayed on a watch (presumably stolen). The hat-box stored over Moll's bed shows that she has formed an association with another newsworthy figure, the highwayman James Dalton who was arrested in December 1729. On the day that Charteris was pardoned in 1730, Dalton was hanged. A letter identifies her as M. Hackabout. Francis Hackabout was condemned for highway robbery in 1730, while his sister Kate was one of the prostitutes detained by the crusading magistrate, Sir John Gonson, in 1730. The fictional Moll is about to share the same fate, since Gonson and his bailiffs are seen entering her room on the right. Her twin heroes are portrayed on the wall in prints: one is the anti-hero of John Gay's *Beggar's Opera*, the highwayman Macheath, and the other is the handsome Tory preacher Dr Henry Sacheverell. Above the bed hang a besom and witch's hat, presumably tools of her trade.

A Harlot's Progress, plate 3,
1732, etching and engraving, 319 x 384 mm

During 1730 the Westminster magistrate Sir John Gonson conducted a crusading purge against the riotous nightlife of the Covent Garden area. People found cruising the street at night were rounded up and brought to him. If they could not account for their behaviour, he sent them off to beat hemp in Tothill Fields Bridewell on the Horseferry Road. He and a group of other magistrates determined to convene every fortnight until they had suppressed the disorderly houses in Westminster. In July warrants were issued against all the brothels around Drury Lane, their keepers were taken into custody and about forty 'lewd women' were sent to beat hemp. Early in August another twenty-two were seized by search warrant and received the same punishment. The purge continued throughout the summer. Pickpockets were also rounded up, and improperly licensed late drinking premises closed. Moll is one such victim of Gonson's unexpectedly determined campaign to clean up and regulate Westminster nightlife.

Detail (see overleaf) of *A Harlot's Progress*, plate 4

Plate 4.

Wm Hogarth inv^t pinx^t et sculp^t

BOTH MOLL and her servant of the previous plate are now in Tothill Fields Bridewell. She, still dressed in incongruously fine clothes, is beating hemp for ropes, whipped on by an overseer while her dress is valued by his wife. A well-dressed gambler has also been picked up and they beat hemp side by side with various less successful petty criminals. Moll's servant, a veteran of the game, is trying on her shoes and stockings.

A Harlot's Progress, plate 4,
1732, etching and engraving, 316 x 386 mm

A Harlot's Progress, plate 5, 1732, etching and engraving, 320 x 390 mm

IN VERY POOR circumstances now, Moll is extremely ill. Dr Rock and Dr Misaubin, both proprietors of patent cures for venereal disease, argue the merits of their respective medicines while Moll's servant points out that their patient is about to expire. Moll's son sits by the fire, while a woman rifles through the professional equipment in her old chest.

A Harlot's Progress, plate 6, 1732, etching and engraving, 316 x 384 mm

MOLL IS IN HER coffin and her son is chief mourner. The priest has his hand up the dress of the woman next to him. Moll's fellow professionals try on the mourning rings and bonnets she has left, their grief fuelled by drink. The inscription on the coffin lid tells us that Moll died at twenty-three.

Think not to find one meant Resemblance there
We lash the Vices but the Persons spare

A MIDNIGHT MODDERN CONVERSATION

Wm Hogarth Inv^t Pinx^t & Sculp^t

A CONVIVIAL GATHERING of respectable gentlemen at the St John's Coffee House, Temple Bar, portrayed at around four in the morning. The clergyman stirring the chinoiserie punchbowl is one of the few still capable of drinking. Other figures are representative of professions or trades. They have been identified as particular individuals, despite the injunction 'Think not to find one meant resemblance there'.

This was the most copied of all Hogarth's subjects. Not only was it plagiarized on prints of all shapes, sizes and prices, but before long it was itself being used as a motif on punchbowls produced in China for the European market.

A Midnight Modern Conversation,
1733, etching and engraving, 341 x 468 mm

For the first time since the passing of the Copyright Act in 1735 Hogarth published a small, relatively cheap print. For a shilling you could have this or the cheapest seat in the theatre. It is comedy rather than satire, though the joke is at the expense of the Church. The preacher's text is 'Come unto me all ye that Labour and are Heavy Laden, and I shall give you Rest', Matthew 11:28. The inscription on the pulpit reads: 'I am afraid of you lest I have bestowed on you labour in vain', Galatians 4:11. Only the preacher and the clerk are awake, but the clerk's attention is fixed on the exposed cleavage of a girl who has fallen asleep with her prayer book open at 'Of Matrimony'. The situation comments on the poor quality of Anglican sermons, while the church decoration conveys Hogarth's opinion of the quality of art in London's churches.

The Sleeping Congregation,
1736, etching and engraving, 263 x 208 mm

Before, 1736, etching and engraving, 405 x 325 mm

After, 1736, etching and engraving, 403 x 328 mm

T HESE PRINTS are libertine rather than moralizing in their appeal.
The girl's diet of Rochester and novels (the latter widely decried
for debauching youth) suggests that her resistance to her suitor is not
very determined. Their prosaic realism makes a striking contrast with
contemporary French *estampes galantes*.

In 1737 the Act Against Strolling Players made it an offence to perform plays without a licence outside London and Westminster. The act specified actors, not actresses, so this company, composed entirely of women and children, evades the rule. They are to perform *The Devil to Pay in Heaven*, and the cast of goddesses and lesser creatures are variously preparing for their parts. The gossip and connoisseur Horace Walpole thought this large print Hogarth's wittiest, many little details appealing to his sense of humour.

Strolling Actresses Dressing in a Barn,
1738, etching and engraving, 428 x 539 mm

A Rake's Progress

Hogarth launched a subscription for *A Rake's Progress* in December 1733 (the ticket opposite is confusing: at that time the year ended in March) and promised to deliver the set the following autumn. In the event he held it back until the Copyright Act came into force and published it the day the Act was passed, 25 June 1735. The price was 1½ guineas to subscribers and 2 guineas after the subscription closed — just under 4s. to subscribers for each plate.

The subscription ticket opposite challenges a common, misconceived assumption that those who could not afford paintings bought prints. His Grace the Duke of Queensberry (as normally spelled), a patron of the author John Gay, was one of many aristocrats who collected Hogarth's prints. In any case Hogarth did not sell the paintings of the *Rake's Progress* until 1745 and, though fine in their way, they cannot be read as clearly as the prints. The printmaking process allowed Hogarth to convey messages through minute details, much of which is also difficult to pick up in reduced reproduction.

The two rakes in the subscription ticket are too concerned with the orange-selling girls to appreciate the jokes on stage, perhaps a wry comment on the idea that his satire could reform real-life rakes. The subscription ticket also reiterates Hogarth's message that his study is nature — real people. His enquiring gaze is directed not at the artifice on stage, but at the audience.

The Laughing Audience (subscription ticket for *Southwark Fair* and *A Rake's Progress*), 1733, etching, 233 x 173 mm

1733 Rec.ᵈ Jan 9 of His Grace the Duke of Quinsburough
Half a Guinea being the first Payment for Nine Prints, 8 of Which
Represent a Rakes Progress & the 9ᵗʰ a Fair. Which I Promise to
Deliver at Michaelmass next on Receiving one Guinea more, the
Print of the Fair being Deliver'd at the time of Subscribing.

TOM RAKEWELL'S father, a very rich and very miserly City banker, has just died. Tom has returned from Oxford University and is being measured for a mourning suit. His day is interrupted by the appearance of his pregnant betrothed, Sarah Young, whom he no longer wishes to marry. In response to her tears and her mother's anger, he offers to buy her off with a handful of gold. His attorney helps himself to the guineas remaining in Tom's dish of loose change. There is money concealed all over the house and clear signs that the merchant has spent precious little on himself.

For this set Hogarth commissioned verses from his friend John Hoadly (1711–76). It was quite common for publishers to commission verses to ornament or explain their prints. These do not tell the story of the prints in detail, but rather muse on it indirectly to derive moral reflections.

A Rake's Progress, plate 1, 1735, etching and engraving, 355 x 410 mm

O Vanity of Age, untoward
Ever Spleeny, ever froward
Why these Bolts, & Massy (a
Squint Suspicions, jealous

At his new residence Tom holds a *Levée* in aristocratic style: a number of people who provide services for the rich attend him as he gets up in the morning in order to press their claims for his patronage. Tom is hiring a rough-looking bodyguard who comes with the recommendation 'the Capt. is a Man of Honour. His sword may serve you'. A jockey presents a bowl won with 'Silly Tom'; a horn player, a French dancing-master and a landscape gardener are next in line. Some at least are meant to portray real people. James Figg is probably the prize-fighter with quarter-staffs and the fencing master is probably Dubois, killed in a duel in 1734. The musician playing the harpsichord is George Handel's rival Nicola Porpora, director of the 'Opera of the Nobility'. Other waiting figures further off include a poet hoping for payment for his dedication of 'An Epistle to Rake'. Tom's taste is indicated by his juxtaposition of two pictures of gamecocks with a 'Judgement of Paris'. Unlike Paris, he has not chosen the most beautiful of his suitors.

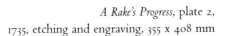

A Rake's Progress, plate 2,
1735, etching and engraving, 355 x 408 mm

Invented & Painted by Wm. Hogarth & Publish'd according to Act of Parliament June ye 25. 1735.   Plate. 2.

...r the unprovided Mind.   Pleasure on her silver Throne   And in their Train, to fill the Press,
...d Memory in fetters bind;   Smiling comes, nor comes alone;   Come apish Dance, and swolen Excess,
...nd faith and Love with golden chain, Venus moves with her along;   Mechanic Honour, vicious Taste,
...sprinkle Lethe o're the Brain!   And smooth Lyæus, ever-young.   And fashion in her changing Vest.

43

IN 1734 a group of aristocrats associated with Frederick Prince of Wales set up a new 'Opera of the Nobility' in rivalry to the existing company directed by George Frideric Handel. Whereas Hogarth's friends were edging Handel towards producing operas in English, the new company was purely Italian. By showering large gifts of money upon them, the Nobility induced a number of the most prominent Italian musicians and singers to come to London. They brought the Neapolitan composer and singing teacher Nicola Porpora (1686–1768) from Venice to be director of the company. He is believed to be the musician depicted here by Hogarth. Porpora composed four operas for the Nobility before returning to Venice in 1736. The aristocrats also secured the services of the alto castrato 'Senesino' (Francesco Bernardi 1686–1758) and of Porpora's star pupil, the soprano castrato Carlo Broschi (1705–82), better known as 'Farinelli', who arrived in London in October 1734.

Porpora is shown with a new opera, *The Rape of the Sabines*, composed specially for the Nobility. It has a cast led by Farinelli as Romulus and the alto castrato Senesino as first Ravisher. The Sabine Women, about to be raped, are also all Italians. Hanging from his chair is a list of the rich presents given to Farinelli by the Nobility. It ends with 'A Gold Snuff box Chac'd with the Story of Orpheus Charming ye Brutes' presented by 'T. Rakewell Esq.'. On the floor is a satirical print showing the Nobility worshipping 'One Gode, One Farinelli'.

The rivalry between the two companies ultimately bankrupted both of them.

Detail of *A Rake's Progress*, plate 2

Tom is having fun in a private room in the notorious Rose Tavern in Drury Lane. The company has amused itself earlier by ripping out the heads of all the Roman emperors except Nero from the set of varnished prints on the wall. Tom sits with a lantern and staff captured from a watchman at his feet. A pretty whore caresses him while relieving him of his watch, which she hands to her colleague. At the table two girls are arguing, two more are drinking heavily, while a fifth entertains Tom's companion. The girl on the right is about to dance naked on the table.

A Rake's Progress, plate 3,
1735, etching and engraving, 355 x 408 mm

of every Houshold Blessing, | Guest Divine to outward Viewing, | With Freedom led to every Part, | To enter in with covert Treason,
harm in Innocence possessing, | Abler Minister of Ruin! | And secret Chamber of y.º Heart; | O'erthrow the drowsy Guard of Reason,
to thy Being, Foe to Love! | And Thou, no less of Gift devine, | Dost Thou thy friendly Host betray, | To ransack the abandon'd Place,
| Sweet Poison of Misused Wine! | And Shew thy riotous Gang y.º way, | And revel there with wild Excess!

Engrav'd, & Publish'd by W.ᵐ Hogarth June y.º 25. 1735. according to Act of Parliment.———

Plate 3.

Tom is *en route* to attend the Queen's Birthday *Levée* at St James's Palace in his finest clothes. St James's Street is crowded with chairs and coaches and a passing Welshman wearing a leek makes it clear that this is 1 March, St David's Day and Queen Caroline's birthday. To his anguished surprise, as he leaves the chair at the corner, Tom is accosted by two bailiffs and arrested for debt. At that moment his jilted sweetheart, Sarah Young, appears offering a purse.

A Rake's Progress, plate 4,
1735, etching and engraving, 356 x 407 mm

oaching views the Harpy Law,
Poverty with icy Paw
vented Painted & Engrav'd by Wm Hogarth, & Publish'd

Ready to seize the poor Remains
That Vice hath left of all his Gains.

Cold Penitence, lame After-Thought,
With Fears, Despair, & Horrors fraught,

Call back his guilty Pleasures dead,
Whom he hath wrong'd, & whom betray'd.

June ye 25. 1735. According to Act of Parliaments.

Plate. 4.

49

A Rake's Progress, plate 5, 1735, etching and engraving, 356 x 407 mm

TOM RESTORES his fortune by marrying a rich widow in Marylebone Church. The ancient one-eyed dame is eager for her ring, but Tom's eye is already on her maid. The hubbub in the background is caused by Sarah Young, her child and mother who are prevented from disrupting the service.

A Rake's Progress, plate 6, 1735, etching and engraving, 352 x 407 mm

Tom loses his money again in a gambling den. All the passions of gambling can be seen in the faces of the players, who are so obsessed they fail to notice the building is on fire. A lord borrows money while a despondent highwayman, seated right, is unimpressed with Tom's passionate despair.

51

Tom is now confined for debt in the Fleet Prison, the fate that had befallen Hogarth's father, Richard, in 1707. He shares a room with two other haggard debtors, both busily attempting to regain their liberty, one through alchemy, the other by designing schemes to repay the National Debt. The manager of Covent Garden Theatre, John Rich, has just returned a play that Tom has written to raise money with the laconic note, 'Sir, I have read your Play & find it will not do'. He is assailed from one side by his reproachful crone of a wife, from the other by demands for payment from the gaoler and a boy runner. Sarah Young, visiting with his child, has fainted in distress.

A Rake's Progress, plate 7,
1735, etching and engraving, 355 x 408 mm

self-approving can review | Not so the Guilty Wretch confin'd. | Talents idle, & unus'd, | Reason the Vessel leaves to steer,
of past Virtues that shine thro' | No Pleasures meet his roving Mind. | And every Gift of Heaven abus'd.— | And gives the Helm to mad Despair.
oom of Age, & cast a Ray, | No Blessings fetch'd from early Youth. | In Seas of Sad Reflection lost, | Invented & by W.ᵐ Hogarth & Publish'd
ld the Evening of his Day! | But broken Faith, & wrested Truth, | From Horrors still to Horrors tost, | According to Act of Parliament June y.ᵉ 25. 1735.

Tom has gone mad and is confined in Bedlam. The patch on his chest shows that he has tried to stab himself and he is being manacled to prevent further self-harm. The location of the scene is confirmed by the manner in which Hogarth has modelled the figures of the Rake and the religious fanatic behind him on the statues that decorated the gate of the Bethlehem Hospital, Moorfields. In the background we see various types of lunatic and two fashionable lady sightseers, much taken with the erect posture of the naked king in cell 55.

Madness, Thou Chaos of y. Br
What art, That Pleasure giv'st, an
Tyranny of Fancy's Reign
Mechanic Fancy; that can t'
Vast Labarynths, & Mazes w'

A Rake's Progress, plate 8,
1735, etching and engraving, 356 x 408 mm

54

Rule disjointed, shapeless Measure.   Shapes of Pleasure, that but seen   The headstrong Course of youth thus run,   See him by Thee to Ruin Sold.
. . .with Horror, fill'd with Pleasure: Wou'd split the shaking Sides of Spleen :   What Comfort from this darling Son :   And curse thy self, & curse thy Gold.
. . .es of Horror, that wou'd even   O Vanity of Age ! here See   His rattling Chains with Terror hear.
. . .Doubt of Mercy upon Heaven.   The Stamp of Heaven efac'd by Thee   Behold Death grappling with Despair;

Invented &c by Wᵐ Hogarth & Publish'd according to Act of Parliament June yᵉ 25. 1735.

THE LINES from Alexander Pope's poem, *The Dunciad*, inscribed beneath *The Distrest Poet*, were directed against the poet and editor Lewis Theobald, but it is unlikely that Hogarth's print had any specific target. Hogarth's poet is, on the whole, a sympathetic figure. His father's experience probably left Hogarth with some compassion for the lonely author, neglected by the all-powerful bookseller-publishers and struggling to support a wife and child.

The poet sits at his desk beside his garret window, hard at work on 'Poverty a Poem'. As a guide he uses Edward Bysshe's *Art of English Poetry*, the most influential and widely used guide to writing poetry in the English language. On the floor lie many rejected drafts, as well as an issue of the *Grub Street Journal*, the long-running satirical parody of newspaper journalism. Above his head is a copy of the print *Veni Vidi Vici* showing Pope beating the bookseller Edmund Curll. His efforts are fuelled by tobacco and snuff.

The family lives in this one garret room in what is probably meant to be Grub Street, the hack writers' ghetto. A small child is crying in the bed. The poet's pretty young wife is patiently mending clothes and babywear is drying before the fire. The cat has made a nest for her kittens on the poet's discarded coat. The cupboard on the wall is bare. The poet's concentration has just been further disturbed by a milkmaid bursting in demanding payment.

Studious he sate, with all his books around, ⟶
Sinking from thought to thought, a vast profund!

Plung'd for his sense, but found no bottom there;
Then writ, and flounder'd on, in mere despair.

DUNCIAD. BOOK I. *line* III.

The Distrest Poet,
1737, etching and engraving, 360 x 410 mm

THE FOUR TIMES OF DAY

COPIES OF Hogarth's paintings of the *Four Times of Day* were commissioned by Jonathan Tyers, proprietor of Vauxhall Gardens, for display in the fashionable pleasure gardens on the river to the south of Westminster.

Morning shows Covent Garden just before seven on a very cold winter's morning, with snow on the rooftops and icicles hanging from the eaves of Tom's Coffee House. Outside this notorious den of iniquity a couple of gentlemen claim the favours of two girls, up early to buy vegetables. Inside, a fight has broken out. A beggar sits beside a fire lit by the frozen market women. A prim, ageing spinster ignores her as she passes with her servant on her way to early morning prayers in St Paul's Church. In the background a crowd gathers around the charlatan Dr Rock, who is selling his venereal cures, causing two schoolboys to pause on their way to school.

Morning,
1738, etching and engraving, 488 x 397 mm

IN *Noon* the scene shifts northwards to the French Huguenot Church in Hog Lane, near Soho Square. We are looking eastwards towards St Giles in the Fields, just after noon in autumn. The well-dressed, sober Huguenot community leaving church contrasts with the English rabble across the alley outside two taverns. From the first floor window of the Silent Woman (silent because headless) a screaming harridan hurls a joint into the street. Beneath the Baptist's Head a black man gropes a wench carrying a pie, causing her to spill the gravy. A boy has broken his plate and a street urchin scrabbles on the floor for the scraps. A fancily dressed Huguenot boy looks approvingly at the dead cat in the gutter.

Noon,
1738, etching and
engraving, 488 x 406 mm

Good Eating

NOON

61

O N A SUMMER Sunday evening a citizen and his family face the long walk home after an afternoon in Islington, to the north of London. They have just left the Sir Hugh Middleton, a pub with tea gardens and a skittle ground. It was named after the philanthropist who channelled the New River, beside them, from Hertfordshire to Clerkenwell, thereby enhancing London's water supply. Behind them is Sadler's Wells theatre. The citizen is a cuckold, to judge from the horns that a trick of perspective places above his head. He carries a sleeping girl who has just lost her shoe, while her brother trails behind whimpering. All of them, including the spaniel, are clearly very hot and tired, especially the pregnant wife.

The distribution of light in this plate, with its distant, fading landscape and wide sunset sky, required engraving skills that Hogarth was not confident he possessed. Consequently he gave the print to Bernard Baron to finish. Baron was a Frenchman who had settled in London and at that time was employed on prints of the gardens at Stowe.

Baron complained to Hogarth that the boy had no cause to whimper, so before publication he added a bullying sister who demands the boy's ginger-bread king. Some parents might consider the walk home to be sufficient cause.

Left: Evening, detail of published state showing the added sister

Evening,
1738, etching and engraving by
Hogarth and Bernard Baron,
480 x 400 mm

This Proof was delivered by Mr. Baron to Mr. Hogarth, it being told him, this boy had no apparent Cause to Whimper, he hit in his Sister threatening him to deliver his Gingerbread King, now he just in Labour. The Character Hogarth, altered where he is Crying

Engraved by Baron
July 13. 1822.

THE NARROWEST POINT in Whitehall, outside the Rummer Tavern, is depicted here, looking north to Le Sueur's statue of Charles I at Charing Cross. It is apparently Restoration Day, 29 May, which celebrated the restoration of Charles II. Windows are illuminated for a night of celebration, people are wearing oak leaf favours and oak leaves bedeck the signs. The Salisbury coach has turned over in avoiding a bonfire in the middle of the street. A huge bonfire burns further off, possibly in Leicester Fields. A freemason staggers home, wearing a collar with a square. He has been

identified as Sir Thomas de Veil, a Westminster magistrate and a member of Hogarth's own first freemason lodge. He is supported by a mason in Tyler's regalia with sword, key and lamp who has been identified as Brother Montgomerie, the Grand Tyler.

Left: Detail of homeless children sheltering under the counter of the barber's shop.

Night,
1738, etching and
engraving, 488 x 397 mm

Invented, Painted, Engraved & Publish'd by Wm Hogarth March 25 1738 According to Act of Parliament

NIGHT

A N ITALIAN MUSICIAN, practising with his violin by an open window, finds himself deafened by the various noises coming from a ballad singer with her crying baby, a parrot, a girl with a rattle watching a boy pissing, an oboe player, a milkmaid, a boy with a drum, a dog barking, a knife grinder, a paviour, a dustman, a sow-gelder blowing his horn, a fish pedlar, and in the distance fighting cats and a chimney sweep on the roof of a pewterer's workshop.

The advertisement on the wall outside his window is for proper English music: a performance of John Gay's enormously popular *Beggar's Opera*.

The Enraged Musician,
1741, etching and engraving, 357 x 412 mm

Marriage A-la-Mode

In April 1743 Hogarth advertised a subscription for 'Six Prints from Copper-Plates, engrav'd by the best Masters in Paris, after his own Paintings, (the Heads for the better Preservation of the Characters and Expressions to be done by the Author) representing a Variety of modern Occurrences in High Life, and call'd Marriage A-la-Mode'. With calculated irony he promised that 'Particular care will be taken that there may not be the least Objection to the Decency or Elegancy of the Whole Work, and that none of the Characters represented shall be Personal'.

Even the advertisement is satirical. The choice of French engravers parodies the usual selection of French engravers for prestigious projects because cultured aristocrats believed they were better. The choice is singularly appropriate for a venture into English high life, which normally aped French manners. In a sarcastic concession to refined sensibilities Hogarth promises nothing indecent or personal.

The series describes a marriage of convenience between the heir of the Earl of Squanderfield and the daughter of a London alderman. The son, Viscount Squanderfield, is more interested in his own reflection, while his bride-to-be falls for Counsellor Silvertongue, her lawyer.

The style of engraving in these prints is finer and flashier than is usual in Hogarth's own. They deliberately parody the most refined of French engravings with a style appropriate to the cosmopolitan aristocracy.

Ultimately, the viscount is poxed by prostitutes. The lawyer seduces the viscountess and kills the viscount in a duel when he surprises them together at a Bagnio. The lawyer is hanged and she commits suicide.

Detail (see overleaf) of *Marriage A-la-Mode*, plate 1

THE GOUTY EARL is immensely proud of his descent from the Conqueror and even his crutch is marked with a coronet. The room is decorated in the French style of Louis XIV and a heroic portrait commemorates the earl's part in Marlborough's wars. The other old masters depict Catholic martyrdoms and classical catastrophes. The earl has spent all his money on building and seeks to restore the family's fortune by marrying his son to money. The merchant wants the social prestige. A Fury on the wall glares down on the incipient liaison between the daughter and the lawyer.

Marriage A-la-Mode, plate 1,
1745, Gérard Scotin, etching
and engraving, 383 x 462 mm

AT 1.20 PM Lady Squanderfield is taking morning tea, having passed most of the night at cards and music. The viscount has just returned from a hard night's dissipation. The dog is excited by the scent of another woman on his coat. The servant is exhausted. The Methodist steward despairs. The Palladian interior of their palace is in William Kent's style, with ludicrous rococo additions. Old master paintings of saints decorate the walls and the mantelpiece is cluttered with antiquities and curiosities.

Marriage A-la-Mode, plate 2, 1745, Bernard Baron, etching and engraving, 385 x 464 mm

Marriage A-la-Mode. (Plate II)

According to Act of Parliament April 1st 1745

AT 7s. 6d., this portrait of the great actor–manager David Garrick (1717–79) was the most expensive print that Hogarth had yet published. It was larger than any previous print of an actor in character and established a market for such portraits. Garrick made his London debut in 1741 as Shakespeare's Richard III and he continued to play the role until his retirement. The playwright Arthur Murphy described how:

> When he started from his dream he was a spectacle of horror. He called forth in a manly voice 'Give me another horse', he paused, and with a countenance of dismay, advanced crying out in a tone of distress 'Bind up my wounds', and then, falling on his knees, said in a most piteous accent, 'Have mercy, Heaven'. In all this the audience saw an exact imitation of nature.

Garrick's expression in Hogarth's portrait (and probably on the stage) was based on the French painter Charles Le Brun's internationally influential treatise for artists on the expression of emotions. Hogarth's print ensured that his friend Garrick's Richard became a national icon, and the alliance between these two great British artists confirmed them both in cosmopolitan esteem.

Mr Garrick in the Character of Richard 3d,
William Hogarth and Charles Grignion, 1746,
etching and engraving, 422 x 530 mm

Painted by W.ᵐ Hogarth.

Publish'd according to Act of Parliam.ᵗ June 20. 17

Mr. Garrick in the Character of Richard the 3.ᵈ

Shakespear. Act 5. Scene 7.

Engrav'd by Wᵐ. Hogarth & C. Grignion.

AT A SHILLING EACH, the twelve prints of *Industry and Idleness* were sold at the standard price for an ordinary print of the middle range. They were aimed at the artisans and tradesmen who formed the middling sort – what would in future be known as the middle class, though there was no such fixed notion of class in Hogarth's day. He adopted a simple, clear style of engraving that was cheaper since quicker to execute. Biblical quotations reinforce the message conveyed through the images.

They tell the contrasting stories of two apprentices, one industrious, the other idle. They are both apprenticed to a Spitalfields silk manufacturer named West. Goodchild, the industrious apprentice, is shown attending church, supervising the manufactory, marrying his master's daughter and going into partnership with him, becoming a sherrif, alderman and finally lord mayor of London. Tom Idle gambles in the churchyard, is turned away and sent into the Royal Navy. Once discharged he is shown sharing a garret with a prostitute. Turning to armed robbery, he is betrayed by his whore, brought before Alderman Goodchild and hanged at Tyburn.

In the fifth plate Tom Idle is being told about naval discipline as he is rowed with his weeping mother along Limehouse Reach to a small man-of-war moored off Deptford Dock. The windmills and gibbet were familiar landmarks.

Industry and Idleness, plate 5,
1747, etching and engraving, 254 x 338 mm

THE 'Four large prints of an Election', as Hogarth listed them, took his prices to a new high. Each cost 10s. 6d., which remained the top price for large prints for about fifteen years. They were, however, very large and very complicated plates. They were published one by one with the first advertised in April 1754. Once again, Hogarth hired help for the landscapes.

The subscription announcement coincided with the General Election of April 1754 and the immediate inspiration for Hogarth's series was the contest for the two Tory-held Oxfordshire seats, which had not been contested since 1710. The University of Oxford was a bastion of Jacobite-leaning Toryism, but parts of the county were violently Whig and the election was extremely close, and spectacularly corrupt and riotous. When the poll took place on 17 April it transpired that only forty-three votes separated the first and last of the four candidates. However, the two Tories, Wenman and Dashwood, were elected.

The general lines of the series may have been inspired by Oxfordshire but beyond the Tory victory the details are not specific to that election where the poll, for instance, took place in the County Court at Oxford. Instead they are generalized and universal in their indictment of the divisive violence and corruption associated with the English electoral process.

This detail, reproduced at the same size as it appears in the original, shows how Hogarth's minute inscriptions operate. Knowing that the Tory candidate is called Tim Parktool, we understand that he is eager to divert election funds to the pretty ladies on the balcony above him in exchange for sexual gratification. The detail also shows how patterns of etched and engraved lines produce different textures and densities of light and shade.

Detail (see overleaf) of 'Four large prints of an Election', plate 2: *Canvassing for Votes*

THIS SERIES takes us on a rare excursion into the English countryside. The farmer in the centre accepts bribes from both parties. The Royal Oak, a Tory Inn, is adorned with a canvas showing the Whig Duke of Newcastle handing out bribes. He was the country's principal controller of patronage. Beneath it the Tory candidate Tim Parktool (see previous page) buys trinkets from a Jewish pedlar in an effort to interest the two attractive ladies on the balcony. A girl who has already been bought counts her reward on a seat that may once have been the figurehead of a warship – certainly, it is the sort of lion that ornamented the king's ships. This one is about to devour a French *fleur-de-lys*.

By the time Hogarth was working on the second plate, the Seven Years War was in progress. The figure on the left outside the Portobello appears to be wearing the 'long clothes' of a seaman. Portobello was a victory won by Admiral Vernon in 1739 after Tory pressure for war.

In the background a Tory mob besieges the Whig pub, The Crown, renamed The Excise Office. While they hurl rocks at the windows, someone shoots at them from inside.

Canvassing for Votes,
1757, Charles Grignion, etching
and engraving, 436 x 566 mm

PLEASE CANDIDATE for GUZZLEDOWN.

...ns Embassador to the Court of RUSSIA. This Plate is most humbly Inscrib'd By his most Obedient humble Servant.

Will.m Hogarth

Published 20.th Feb.y 1757. As the Act directs.

I N 1748 Hogarth visited Paris. By his own account, as he was returning through Calais he was arrested while sketching one of the medieval gates which was still decorated with the English coat of arms. This print is set at the moment of his arrest. Just behind the artist to the left of the gate can be seen the halberd and hand of the sergeant arresting him on suspicion of spying. The rest is a calculated insult to the French. The Bourbon soldiers at the gate in their ragged white uniforms have just been issued their *soup maigre* and two men wearing slavish clogs struggle with the weight of the cauldron. Through the gate are glimpsed peasants kneeling for passing priests. Two barefooted peasants pause to admire a huge fish held by a third woman. All the Frenchmen are emaciated with the exception of a fat friar who paws greedily at the central motif of the picture, a huge piece of English beef being carried by a staggering servant from the port to the English hotel run by Mme Grandsire. A starving highlander, in exile after the 1745 rebellion, sits in the foreground.

The title is lifted from a famous song written by Hogarth's friend Henry Fielding, 'The Roast Beef of Old England', which lamented the bad influence of effeminate French customs and food in diluting English manliness.

O The Roast Beef of Old England,
William Hogarth and Charles Mosley, 1749,
etching and engraving, 382 x 458 mm

The March to Finchley shows George II's troops marching north from London to oppose the Jacobite army of Charles Edward Stuart. They have reached Tottenham Court turnpike where some of the relatives and cheering onlookers will turn back. The troubled grenadier at the centre faces a Choice of Hercules between Vice and Virtue. He is simultaneously urged onward by a pregnant hawker with a print of the general, the Duke of Cumberland, and dragged backward by a Catholic crone wielding *The Jacobite Journal*. His drummer tries to get him moving, but he is being held back by his grief-stricken wife and son. The fusiliers are falling out to kiss, steal and drink, and a furious sergeant tries to whip them in. The madam of a brothel prays for the army's safe return.

According to Hogarth, George II refused his dedication on the grounds that the print showed his troops as ill-disciplined, so he dedicated it instead to the king of Prussia.

The March to Finchley,
Luke Sullivan, 1750, etching
and engraving, 431 x 554 mm

A Representation of the March of the Guards towards Scotland, in the Year 1745.   Engrav'd by Luke Sullivan.

KING of PRUSIA, an Encourager of ARTS and SCIENCES!   This Plate is most humbly Dedicated.

Hogarth advertised engravings of the *Four Stages of Cruelty* together with *Beer Street* and *Gin Lane* in February 1751. He told readers that 'As the Subjects of these Prints are calculated to reform some reigning Vices peculiar to the lower Class of People in hopes to render them of more extensive Use, the Author has published them in the cheapest Manner possible'. It appears that a pair of woodcuts dated January 1750 preceded the engravings of *Cruelty*. Woodcuts were the prints that the labouring classes generally bought since they could be printed in huge editions and consequently retailed for a penny each or less. Hogarth's attempt to publish woodcuts may have failed since only two of the four stages appeared in this form. If so, the problem was probably distribution. Having cut the printsellers who controlled the retail networks for wide distribution out of the market for his other prints, they may have refused their help. Hogarth's normal method of advertising prints to be bought from his house could not possibly attract the mass audience he needed for the sort of propagandist exercise he envisaged. Even at a shilling each, the engravings were too expensive to reach 'the lower Class of People', although their display in public places might have had some effect.

The *Four Stages of Cruelty* describe the career of Tom Nero, a child of the slum parish of St Giles, who begins by torturing dogs, progresses to horses, murders his pregnant lover and is ultimately dissected by surgeons as an executed criminal. In *Cruelty in Perfection* Nero has been seized after murdering the servant Ann Gill, even though she has unwillingly done his bidding by robbing her mistress.

Cruelty in Perfection,
John Bell, 1750, woodcut,
453 x 380 mm

87

Beer Street and *Gin Lane* (overleaf) are a pair, contrasting the virtues of wholesome English beer with the pernicious effects of cheap spirits. They were published in support of the campaign led by Henry Fielding and his brother for the Gin Act passed in summer 1751. The Fielding brothers, both magistrates, linked gin-drinking with a rise in robbery.

We are back in the familiar streets of London. Outside the Barley Mow a cooper lifts a foaming quart tankard with one hand and a French postillion with the other. A jolly butcher laughs. The war with France has just ended and they have been reading the papers with the king's speech recommending the cultivation of commerce and the arts of peace. Two fishwives, one with another quart tankard, read a ballad in favour of the herring fishery by Hogarth's friend John Lockman. The poor pawnbroker can only afford a pint, but across the street roadmenders refresh themselves as do two chairmen, who pause in their carriage of a large lady. Even the tilers working on a rooftop can afford to drink beer. On the right a basket of books consigned for waste paper to line trunks includes volumes in favour of Royal Societies, ancient painting, old masters and politics.

Only the artist who touches up the sign of the Barley Mow is still dressed in rags, cheerful despite being unable to afford a drink.

Beer Street,
1751, etching, 383 x 325 mm

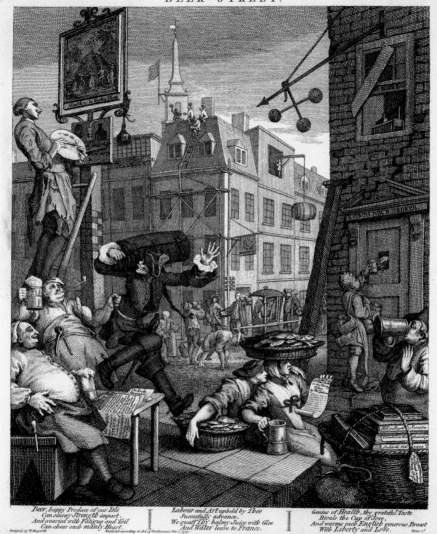

Beer, happy Produce of our Isle
Can sinewy Strength impart,
And wearied with Fatigue and Toil
Can chear each manly Heart.

Labour and Art upheld by Thee
Successfully advance,
We quaff Thy balmy Juice with Glee
And Water leave to France.

Genius of Health, thy grateful Taste
Rivals the Cup of Jove,
And warms each English generous Breast
With Liberty and Love.

Designed by W. Hogarth   *Published according to Act of Parliament Feb. 1. 1751.*   *Price 1.*

Gin Lane is set in the impoverished parish of St Giles where 30,000 people were crammed into slum dwellings and it was said that in 1750 every fourth house was a gin shop. St George's Bloomsbury can be seen over the rooftops.

The source of evil is the gin cellar bottom left. Over its cavernous door is the inscription 'Drunk for a Penny Dead drunk for two pence Clean Straw for Nothing'. A cadaverous ballad singer has passed out on the steps, still clutching bottle and glass. He should be selling 'The Downfall of Madam Gin'. A ragged woman above is oblivious to her child's plunge over the edge of the steps. Gripe the pawnbroker is thriving, as people pawn everything for drink. The coffin maker and Kilman the distiller are also doing well. Other buildings are in a state of ruin. A barber has hanged himself for want of business. Mothers quieten their babies with gin and children sip it. 'What must become of the Infant who is conceived in Gin', wrote Henry Fielding in 1751, 'with the poisonous Distillations of which it is nourished both in the Womb and at the Breast?' The only people working are the burial parties.

Gin Lane,
1751, etching, 379 x 319 mm

GIN LANE.

Gin cursed Fiend, with Fury fraught.
    Makes human Race a Prey.
It enters by a deadly Draught.
    And steals our Life away.

Virtue and Truth, driv'n to Despair.
    It's Rage compells to fly.
But cherishes with hellish Care.
    Theft, Murder, Perjury.

Damn'd Cup! that on the Vitals preys.
    That liquid Fire contains
Which Madness to the Heart conveys.
    And rolls it thro' the Veins.

THIS IS THE first state of a print that was extensively altered before it was published in 1762 as *Credulity, Superstition and Fanaticism*. It is an elaborate satire on Methodism, a fashionable movement within the Church of England that was gaining ground, especially among the common people.

The preacher is George Whitefield. His Harlequin shirt identifies him as a charlatan, his wig has fallen off to reveal the tonsure of a Jesuit. Methodism was commonly condemned as promoting the worst excesses of Popery. Whitefield uses puppets taken from famous old master paintings to make his point. The congregation is comforted and nourished by manifestations of Christ's presence. The notorious bawd Mother Douglas is in convulsions. Such happenings were commonplace when Whitefield spoke: as John Wesley noted in 1739, 'no sooner had he begun (in the application of his sermon) to invite all sinners to believe in Christ, than four persons sunk down close to him, almost in the same moment. One of them lay without either sense or motion; a second trembled exceeding; the third had strong convulsions all over his body, but made no noise, unless by groans ...'. A Turk looks on in astonishment.

The handwriting is Hogarth's own. The most notable change before publication was the alteration of the Christ figures to models of the Cock Lane Ghost, a notorious rigged haunting. Taste, or even the danger of prosecution, may have caused Hogarth to tread cautiously.

'Enthusiasm Delineated',
c. 1761, etching and engraving, 375 x 326 mm

93

HOGARTH MADE THIS print as a 'Tail-Piece' to end volumes of his collected works. It contains a series of bleak images of the end of time with no prospect of renewal. Time dies, gasping 'Finis' and clutching his will, which bequeaths all and every atom to Chaos, his sole executor.

The image also contains Hogarth's last obstinate word in support of his controversial theoretical treatise, *The Analysis of Beauty*, and his final assault on his inveterate enemies, the 'Dealers in Dark Pictures'.

The Bathos,
1764, etching and engraving, 318 x 336 mm

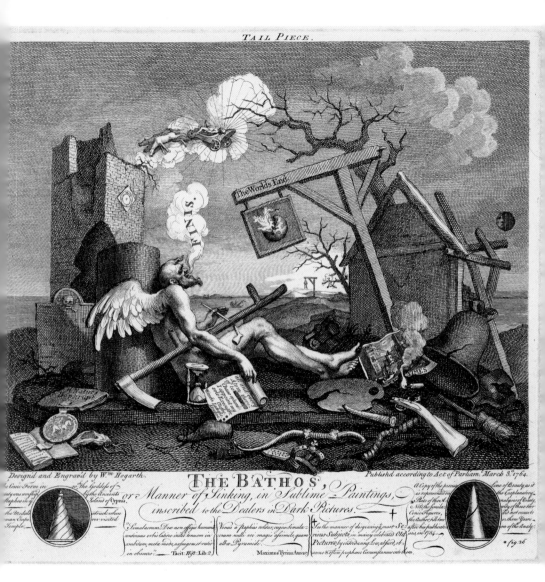

95

ILLUSTRATION REFERENCES

Photographs © The Trustees of the British Museum, courtesy of the Departments of Prints and Drawings and of Photography and Imaging.